This book belongs to:

_____

_____

ANIMALS OF THE AFRICAN SAVANNAH
DAYTIME

Vervet monkey

Striped ground squirrel

Common agama

Klipspringer

African sacred ibis

Masai giraffe

Rufous elephant shrew

Hippopotamus

Lesser flamingo

Cheetah

Patas monkey

African buffalo

Helmeted guineafowl

Common eland

Grey crowned crane

Goliath heron

Ostrich

Thomson's gazelle

Beautiful sunbird

African wild dog

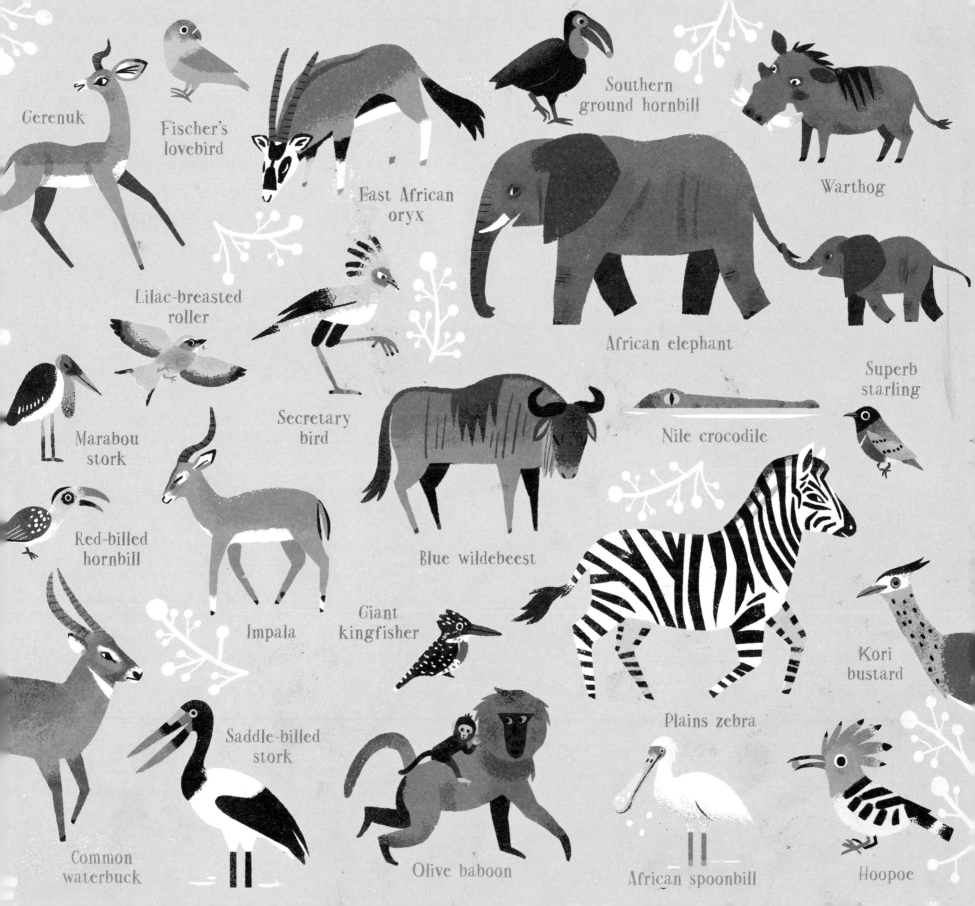

Gerenuk

Fischer's lovebird

East African oryx

Southern ground hornbill

Warthog

African elephant

Lilac-breasted roller

Secretary bird

Superb starling

Marabou stork

Nile crocodile

Red-billed hornbill

Blue wildebeest

Impala

Giant kingfisher

Plains zebra

Kori bustard

Common waterbuck

Saddle-billed stork

Olive baboon

African spoonbill

Hoopoe

For my parents

One Day on Our Blue Planet: In the Savannah © Flying Eye Books 2015.

This paperback edition published in 2019. First published in 2015 by Flying Eye Books, an imprint of Nobrow Ltd. 27 Westgate Street, London, E8 3RL.

All characters, illustrations and text © Ella Bailey 2015.
Ella Bailey has asserted her right under the Copyright, Designs and Patents Act, 1988, to be identified as the Author of this Work.

1 3 5 7 9 10 8 6 4 2

Published in the US by Nobrow (US) Inc.
Printed in Poland on FSC® certified paper.

MIX
Paper from
responsible sources
FSC® C002795

ISBN: 978-1-911171-76-8

www.flyingeyebooks.com

Ella Bailey

ONE DAY
ON OUR
BLUE PLANET

...IN THE SAVANNAH

Flying Eye Books
London | New York

As the morning sun rises on the African savannah, a lioness and her cub emerge slowly from their secret den.

Since this cub's birth, his mother has kept him safe and hidden.
Now he is big and ready to join the rest of his family,
who all live together in a group called a pride.

These are his aunts...

...and these are his cousins.

This is the father of all the cubs. He is very, very big...

...and his roar is very, very loud.

The lions share their home with many other strange and wonderful creatures.
The little cub chases his mother's tail through the tall grass...

...to the river for a cool drink, as midday is when the fiery sun burns hottest. Water is very precious on the savannah, sometimes it may not rain for months and months.

Adult lions are very good at relaxing,
and can spend most of their day sleeping...

...but this little cub is best at playing!

He loves nothing more than hunting
and growling and stalking and chasing.

The sun begins to set and the air grows cooler.
The lionesses leave the cubs in a safe place.

Now it is time to hunt!

They work together to get closer ... and closer
... and closer...

...to their prey.

While some animals eat plants, and others eat insects,
a lion's favourite food is meat.

This little lion cub is still very small and
so for now he only needs his mother's milk.

Lions often stay awake during the night,

but this cub has had a very long day...

...so he sleeps under the cool light of the moon...

...until the sun rises once again, on another day on our blue planet.

ANIMALS OF THE AFRICAN SAVANNAH
NIGHT-TIME

White-tailed
mongoose

Hooded
vulture

Striped
hyena

Caracal

African savanna hare

Leopard

Aardvark

Ground pangolin

Aardwolf

Black-backed jackal

Bat-eared fox

South African
springhare

Yellow-billed duck

African civet

Crested porcupine

Serval

Verreaux's eagle-owl

Straw-coloured fruit bat

Senegal bushbaby

White-backed vulture

Common genet

Spotted hyena

Bushbuck

Black rhinoceros

If you liked this, you'll love...

Hardback ISBN: 978-1-909263-67-3

Hardback ISBN: 978-1-911171-08-9

Hardback ISBN: 978-1-911171-41-6

Check out these other titles from Ella Bailey's bestselling series to find out what life is like for more adorable creatures in their corners of our blue planet.

www.flyingeyebooks.com